AGE BRINGS THEM HOME TO ME

poems by

windflower

Finishing Line Press
Georgetown, Kentucky

AGE BRINGS THEM HOME TO ME

For Linda, whose heart is my home

Copyright © 2024 by windflower
ISBN 979-8-88838-471-8 First Edition
All rights reserved under International and Pan-American Copyright Conventions.
No part of this book may be reproduced in any manner whatsoever without written permission from the publisher, except in the case of brief quotations embodied in critical articles and reviews.

ACKNOWLEDGMENTS

Grateful acknowledgment is given to the editors of the following publications, in which poems in this book have been previously published or are forthcoming, sometimes in different form:

Beyond Words. "Breathing in the Darkness" "My Grandfather Was Precise"
Inner Eye, Anthology. "It is the women who"
Sinister Wisdom. "She said" "A Beginning with No End"
The Persimmon Tree. "She stood at the second floor window"
Tiny Seed Literary Journal. "Canoe me into the deep waters"
Writers of the Mendocino Coast Anthologies. "Mapping" "Young Woman with a Water Pitcher"

I would like to give credit to Mark Smith Soto for the title of my book which is a phrase from his poem "Reflection: Them, Me."

A deep appreciation goes to all the women who have encouraged my writing over the years, both in and out of my writing groups. With a special thanks to Zo Abell, Maureen Eppstein, Harriet Gleeson, Carmen Goodyear, H.A. Hyder, Suzanne Lewis, Susan Lundgren, Joycelyn Trigg and Laurie York. And a very special thanks to Susan Hagen, Kirsten Miles, Susan Tyler and Elizabeth Kirkpatrick-Vrenios.

This book would not have been possible without the wise and insightful feedback of Kristina Marie Darling.

And always, my heart filled thanks to my wife, Linda Shear, for her inspiration, careful eye and abundant love.

Publisher: Leah Huete de Maines
Editor: Christen Kincaid
Cover Art: windflower Townley
Author Photo: Linda Shear
Cover Design: Elizabeth Maines McCleavy

Order online: www.finishinglinepress.com
also available on amazon.com

Author inquiries and mail orders:
Finishing Line Press
PO Box 1626
Georgetown, Kentucky 40324
USA

Contents

Prologue Poem 1

Section One
Ancestry of Geography 3
I am from the ocean 4
A Streetcar Named Desire 5
My father came over in the belly 6
Breathing in the Darkness 7
She said 8
My Grandmother's Hands 9
My Grandfather Was Precise 10
She stood at the second floor window 11

Section Two
Ancestry of Geography 13
Mapping 14
Seeds of Fear 15
Fifty Five Miles to Go 16
Canoe me into deep waters 17
Looking for Signs 18
Close to the Bone 19
A Beginning with No End 20
Primetta Piccini 21
One Step Ahead of Grief 22
I know I should be of use 23

Section Three
Ancestry of Geography 25
The ocean is always talking 26
It is the women who 27
Young Woman with a Water Pitcher 28
Long Night's Day 29
Again, a dream of elephants 30
My First History Lesson 31
Storm Over White Canyon 36

Prologue Poem

This book is a gift to the seven year old girl who placed her first poem in the white and tan porcelain perfume bottle. Its reflection rests beside her own on a filigree gold mirrored tray dead center on her French provincial vanity. Rolled so tight to slip through the narrow neck.

What did I imagine then?

Did I imagine I would be writing about my mother's pink azalea bush, my mother's hands as they made buttery sugared crumbs for her coffee cakes? Or would I be writing about my grandmothers' hands sewing, playing the tambourine, creating a hundred variations of cat's cradle? Or the water haunting my writing from the Atlantic Ocean to the Pacific?

I couldn't fathom writing about my 10th grade biology teacher's son being murdered in Mississippi for registering Black voters. I certainly couldn't imagine my father's brain tumor the size of a grapefruit leaving me to look for his smile on the lines of my brother's faces. Nor could I imagine the cornflower blue rivers of Linda's eyes.

What I can imagine now is acknowledging that child who loved words, a woman who follows a path of vowels and consonants down to the ocean, who won't let hope slip away with the king tides. A woman who has found a cathedral in nature that blesses her with endless images among the broken shells and polished stones; the cool morning dew draped along the branches; the slash of pale blue dawn settling around her like a cloak. Those places where joy lives.

Let us find joy in the voices of people rising up like my grandmother's sweetbread on a cold bitter day. Let us take joy to go wherever we find it: beside the shadows, inside the holes, behind the doors, under our dreams, alongside the air we breathe.*

---

*Credit the concept of joy to go from the poem *Let us take this joy to go* by January Gill O'Neil.

Follow the path of constellations
woman in the sky clothed in sun
moon under her feet

Ancestry of Geography

I spent my first nine summers
on one of Long Island's many islets
on the hem of
                                      New Rochelle
crossing the water in an open ferry

                            jumping onto the landing

up the long slatted ramp
to the upper dock

  falling

            falling

     between   the   upward   ramp

                        and the dock on stilts

I am from the ocean

before I knew the taste
of ocean brine
the bruise of barnacles
against my palm

before I knew the call
of sea shells
the tiny tongues of sand
between my toes

before I knew the pillars
of sun seeping through water
the moist chiffon of fog
grazing my face

before I knew the seduction
of wind poppies
purple sand verbena
reaching for my ankles

I am from the ocean
of my mother's womb
that liminal space:

A Streetcar Named Desire

Maybe it was the sudden melting of snow
across Central Park in mid-February
snow that had held tight to the earth
as my parents held tight to each other
in those first months of marriage
watching the golden crown of autumn
turn to frost thirsty for each other
in their apartment on Williams Bridge Road
the false promise of spring.
Eleven minutes and 2.6 miles from Broadway
I took my first breath in early December
Marlon Brando and Jessica Tandy
heating up the cold winter's night
I wasn't planned and yet there I was
with the shouts of "Stella" "Stella"
welcoming me into the world.

My father came over in the belly

of my grandmother   in the belly
of the ship   open skies
and symphonic air trailing behind

My father would have been one hundred if

>He hadn't started smoking
>those damn Lucky Strikes
>when he was twelve

>Going to college hadn't meant
>changing his name Citarella to Townley
>leaving melting timbres of music behind

>The Navy hadn't inked that
>anchor tattooed on his arm
>swinging wildly unmoored
>through storms of torpedoes

>He'd spent more time in a pew
>on summer Sundays
>rather than swimming with us kids
>or playing gin rummy

>Instead of ice cream and dental supplies
>put his ear to the ground
>listening for the hooves of wild horses
>and time had not been a thief of verses

If the tumor the size of a grapefruit
had not burrowed into his brain
no sections of sweetness   only acid
burning the words from his lips

Breathing in the Darkness

It's November 3, 1957. The Soviet Launch of the Sputnik 2. On board is Laika, the first animal to orbit earth. A Siberian Husky rescued from the streets of Moscow. They assume as a stray she has learned to endure harsh conditions. After two days and fifteen orbits around earth her life support system gives out. She continues to circle the earth for five months until the space ship burns up like a meteor and her spirit is set free.

It's June 1959. My father brings home a 70 pound brindled boxer with floppy ears. He is powerful and playful and too strong for us to walk. We don't have him long enough to miss him. It's September 1959 by father brings home a mixed mutt with long hair. My mother doesn't want all that hair in the house. No more dogs are brought home that year or any other year my father is alive.

It's July 20, 1969. The men land on the moon. My father says when he dies he wants his body released in space. It is hot and we are standing on the gray flagstone patio breathing in the darkness and the curved light. The sweep of night air across my face reminds me of a moonless clear night 18 years ago, he is reaching up holding the stars with one hand and me with the other.

It's October 1979. My father, dead for 10 years. A psychic predicts he will send me a dog.

It's May 1980. My father sends me a yellow lab I rescue from the streets of Amherst Massachusetts. She is mine to keep.

It's August 2019. My two border collies are howling at the waxing crescent moon. I look up into the fading black blanket of dawn, and see brilliant Sirius, the dog star.

She said

Sitting on a cold
linoleum floor
refusing.

My mother told me what
matters. Best not to wear that
skirt too short. Get that hair
out of your eyes. Keep your opinions
to yourself. Men don't like
smart women.

She said it would kill
my grandma. Loving another
woman.

My Grandmother's Hands

On the cap rail
four children gathered
one in your belly
leaving behind
vineyards orchards and pastures
the Amalfi Coast

Your tambourine rattling stories
jingling sparkling
over 4000 miles
to the backyard Bronx brownstone
your quick light steps flirt
with purple and red heirloom tomatoes

Balls of string tumbling in the drawer
    fox and a whale   fly on a nose
fish in a dish   pigs on a peg
    owl's eyes   raven's feet
a hundred variations
    of cat's cradle

                My head leans in
                rests against your belly
                your hands veined like crystal blue seas
                flow across my forehead
                I imagine the sixteen year old girl
                embroidering lace on pillowcases
                hands stilling the waves

My Grandfather Was Precise

White shirt, tie and cufflinks.
Red wine for lunch
rolling the grapes from his youth
around a tongue
still heavy with another language.
The wool chestnut color coat
deep brown velvet collar against my chin
me turning this way and that
sleeves, hem, buttons
one stitch at a time
the needle in his hand.
Candescent brown chestnuts
his fingers find the scores
tiny as sparrow's feet.
He removes shell and skin
gives birth to the nutty flavor
earthy and sweet soft and buttery
like those moments
he pulls a silver dollar from his pocket
and places it in my hand.

She stood at the second floor window

mouth full of clothespins
my two small hands
lifting the wet laundry
out of the basket
piece by piece
our offering to every
bead of morning light
wedged within the courtyard
a stain glassed basilica
straining to fill the rectangular
kitchen window
her small frame bending
her hands sculpting
lasagna and manicotti
ricotta cheesecakes
and warm chestnut pies
the taste of centuries
held in the lips
of clothespins

We saw stars hanging on trees
felt rain filling the spaces
between bones

Ancestry of Geography

A lake once lived
under my tag and hopscotch street
             flowing
beneath my mother's pink azalea bush
my father's attempt at tomatoes
the backyard fence
I climbed late to school
A portal to the past opens
into an undercurrent of memories

             swimming
in the wide-skirted navy gown
of the Atlantic where Swianoy
birch bark canoes were once thrones
upon the waterways

Mapping

Beneath my skin
the shallows
of New England

Sizzling summers
of low tide
jellyfish starfish and crab
swimming floating
seaweed surfing
into high tide

But just as
night waves
through tall grasses
in distant prairies

It is here
among the redwoods
where the coast uncurls
her craggy palm
and wildflowers glow
in lullabied light

Shadows of birds
drift across this red stained sky
of rising moons and setting suns

Seeds of Fear

Sown when I was young taking root in the dark confessional booth. A steel wire window between me and forgiveness. Years of Sunday sermons, Wednesday catechisms burrowing into the soil of my spirit.

Afraid to sleep at night. Each lie and omission an invitation to the devil. Rosary beads like burn scars on my hands.

Night voices from downstairs scurry around me. I leave my bed for the stairway landing. Look through the thin white painted bars. Wait for the midnight air to pull the guests into its shadows. Quiet. In bare feet I walk down the shiny wooden stairs calling to my parents. The concern in their brown eyes, the color of mine, draw me closer. The trinity of us huddle on the dusty pink couch in absolution of love.

Fifty Five Miles to Go

Soon this rain will turn me to snow
All in white riding over mountains
Early evening eyes almost closed icy roads
A bird balanced on a half open window

All in white riding over mountains
No brakes one hand on the wheel
A bird balanced on a half open window
Nimbus clouds fading into sleet

No brakes one hand on the wheel
Downpour seeping through windows
Nimbus clouds fading into sleet

Downpour seeping through windows
Driving my car straight up into sky
I want to be a bird taking flight into yellow hills
Rear view mirror floating down river

Canoe me into the deep waters

rain me to the ground,
light breeze me along
the lips of river's currents,
thunderstorm me lightening
my bones to stars,
serenade me with sweet corn
salty butter dripping
from my mouth.
Succulent summer wrap
sweet blueberry arms
around me;
tickle me taunt me trick me
into believing this myopicy is all there is
a calico bonnet filled
with meadows of purple poppies
a celestial cradle filled with bears and dragons
sea goats and swans.
Make me your summer lullaby
my hair a nest for red winged blackbirds
my fingers Queen Anne's lace and little star asters.

Looking for Signs

Then I met you
a journey on water
with wild horses the color of your hair

The new ways of seeing winter skies
light falling across my own terrain
our dogs' breaths melting the snow
smiles dripping from their mouths

We became our own compass
the full moon a guide
across the creek of untethered desires
our fingers excavators mining

your hand a breakwater upon my back
my breath rising tides against your skin

Close to the Bone

Seventy years rubbing
against femur
titanium and ceramic
closer to the bone than
my own hip.
What happens
to thousands of days
etched into marrow
ribbons of coastlines
acres of forest floors
miles clocked
dogs by my side
or when we danced
at our wedding.
When the doctor removes my hip
I will smell
the salt on the craggy fingers
of the Pacific
the thin arms of wisteria hanging
along the Amalfi Coast.

A Beginning with No End

I left the ice hanging from branches
like the crawling creaking
of reclaimed barn board in the wind
freezing the locks of cars.
The home where we began to make a life
together that frigid first winter
with its Plexiglas windows and hollow core door
our coats frozen statues on hooks
against its flimsy back,
our dogs bounding out the door
into the full force of February
returning with eyelashes glistening like diamonds.
Stars leaning into dawn
our waterbed a boat in its own warm harbor
our crisp breath against the bedroom air
our flushed breath against each other's bodies.

                    These same bodies thirty eight years later
                    living on the Mendocino Coast, cliffs
                    painted with purple ice plants
                    tidal pools of sun drenched sea stars,
                    still remember all the love held
                    in eleven hundred square feet
                    where we first plumbed the depths of our
                    desires
                    kisses that melted glaciers
                    kisses that know neither season nor coast.

Primetta Piccini

Purple kerchief around her head
wisps of gray shining in the sun
hands large generous calloused
resting on a cane
white bucket at her feet
filled with brown nylon stockings
instead of chicken feed

Harvesting wheat in the copper hills
Tuscany grain shattering skin
sun punishing neck husband bent over
daughter skipping through fields
into folds of Florence

Centuries worn cobblestones
beneath our feet
a clothesline and an ocean
of language between us
she points to the sky
bella luna bella luna
our smiles two ships
on the same sea

One Step Ahead of Grief

Watching the sun awaken from slumber
lazily layered light reminding me
we made it through another night

I watch the silence between bare branches
one tree in full fall foliage
against the cracked open slate sky

I know I should be of use

Ferrying port to port. Memories
of jars, glass, gold and spices. My rusty hull
home to barnacles.

But what about those days I just want
to be a leaf on a bough. Waiting
to turn red.

Rust in the river

Ancestry of Geography

The green house on Hertford Street
                        haunting my dreams
drifting from room to room
my feet rising
                        and falling

along the lip of ocean's tides

The ocean is always talking

even when I don't
hear it. The sand I find on my
closet floor. The salt
on the dog's purple collar. The way
a wisp of blue brushes
across the sky.

It is the women who

look up at the sky
and see their children
nestled in the moon.

take the map of the world
in their hands
and hold it like Venetian glass.

sing wild horses
to a sanctuary away
from herding helicopters.

roam the woods
counting mushrooms
to feed the world.

walk for miles feet bare
children in their arms
stand side by side-a battered fence.

It is the women who
hem the skirt of the ocean.

Young Woman with a Water Pitcher
    1662-Johannes Vermeer

A young woman by a window
a gold-plated pitcher
in one hand matched
by the flare of sunlight
caressing her other
a map rests
on the wall behind her

                      He would like to approach

                      but kept at a distance

                      perhaps by the table between them
                              perhaps by the primary colors

She daydreams
forgetting the pitcher
in her hand
following the flare of light
out the window

Long Night's Day

Force of fire steam through the windows
Yellow of the sun red of Mars she wears the shawl
The evening balances on a waxing silver crescent

Force of fire steam through the windows
A butterfly takes flight across the world
The evening balances on a waxing silver crescent
Second sight whale swimming through deep water

The butterfly takes flight across the world
Pure white swans skim lightly past each other
Second sight whale swimming through deep water
Soft blues and greens in watery calm

Swans skim lightly past each other
Silver cup the vessel the chalice the grail
The flight of an eagle through a dragonfly's breath

Again, a Dream of Elephants

Ears shaped like the continent of Africa
walking the Savana plains,
three calves in the shadow
of their mama's belly
sheltered from the blistering sun,
the promise of rain and mud
hidden in their furrowed skin.

Her trunk rests in the palm of my hand.
Placing my forehead against this
primordial appendage
I ask forgiveness.

My First History Lesson

one Black college student from Meridian
two white Jews from New York
three civil rights workers
    James Chaney   Andrew Goodman   Michael Schwerner
working to register Black voters

*Quite a few of the student invaders have preconceived
notions about Mississippi.*
                              Tom Ethridge, Jackson Clarion-Ledger

April 24, 1964

charring the landscape
    twenty burnt out churches
        sixty one simultaneous cross burnings
      ten thousand KKK
        crosses caked with rust
Mississippi burning for freedom

*…uncalled for invasion of a sovereign state by a bunch of
Northern students schooled in causing trouble
under the guise of bringing 'freedom' to Mississippi Negros.*
                                    Dallas Morning News

June 16. 1964

sun long set
they came hunting for Schwerner
at the Mount Zion Baptist Church
lined up military fashion with rifles and shotguns
(he wasn't there)
they pounced on the three Black women
and seven Black men leaving the meeting

four hundred years of hate
squeezed into a red ten gallon can
poured inside the church
a million fireballs
exploding into the sky

...the really serious aspect of this invasion...is (that it) is part of an overall-all scheme to destroy the United States by the way of a racial revolution.
Lowell Liberator

June 21, 1964

the sun rose as usual
ninety three degrees at high noon
they visited the remains
of Neshoba County's Mount Zion Baptist Church
never returning to weeping mothers

> Fannie Lee Chaney
> (baker, vandalized and firebombed, civil rights activist)
>
> Carolyn Goodman
> (clinical psychologist, agitator for justice, witness for the prosecution)
>
> Anne Schwerner
> (my biology teacher, salt and pepper hair, outspoken unwavering)

four pm
ninety seven degrees inside and out
of their blue Ford station wagon
stopped for speeding
arrested for arson

Waiting for the Mississippi sun to go down

deputy sheriff locked them up for six hours
denied paying fines
denied making a phone call

Waiting for the Mississippi sun to go down

they worked for Congress of Racial Equality
(CORE) made a call to the jail at five thirty
later denied by police but records revealed

Something happened after the Mississippi sun went down

released under an eighty degree waxing gibbous moon
kept driving south to Meridian
not on the narrow unpaved road
but Highway 16 to Highway 19
deputy sheriff and friends not far behind
stars began to fall

*Well boys you've done a good job. You've struck a blow
for the white man. Mississippi can be proud of you.
Go home and forget it. But before you go, I'm looking
each one of you in the eye and telling you this: The first man
who talks is dead.*
Deputy Sheriff Cecil Ray Price

June 23, 1964

still smoldering…
molten metal melting…
station wagon found
        near the Bogue Chitto Swamp

I don't believe there's three missing, I believe it is a publicity stunt.
    Senator James Eastland to President Lyndon Johnson

Those boys are in Cuba.
    Mississippi Governor Paul Johnson to President Lyndon Johnson

July, 1964

two full moons come and go
investigators comb
the woods, fields and swamps
pushing through dust
        mud
        water
Pearl River weeds dragged
finding remains of eight African American men
lives lost forgotten fighting for freedom

*The slaying of a Negro in Mississippi is not news,
it is only because my husband and Andrew Goodman*

are white that the national alarm has been sounded.
Rita Schwerner

Johnson tapes a call he makes to FBI head J. Edgar Hoover:

JOHNSON: *I saw this Mrs. Schwerner this evening.*
HOOVER: *Yeah.*
JOHNSON: *The wife of the missing boy.*
HOOVER: *Yeah. She's a communist, you know.*
JOHNSON: *No, but she acted worse than that.*
HOOVER: *Is that so?*
JOHNSON: *Yeah, she was awfully mean and very ugly. ... She wants thousands of extra people put down there ...*

August 4, 1964

an anonymous tip
three bodies in a red-clay earthen dam
I got a dam big enough to hold a hundred of them.

Schwerner and Goodman
one shot in the heart
Chaney
three shots
beaten
broken
castrated

their bodes chilled against the clay

After the Mississippi sun went down

red hot and cool ice-blue stars
fell down on Rock Cut Road

August 7, 1964

ten men   coconspirators
  two sheriffs
    pastor
      business owner

    police officer
      commercial driver
        salesman
          mechanic
            cattle farm owner
              honorably discharged Marine

their bloody hands
hollowed stars from the sky
and the moon went mad

Storm Over White Canyon

in memory of Tanya Humphries
February 9, 1980-September 14, 1996

Is that my father's red truck
grit against the window
driving down dusty UT 95
humble Abajo mountains
at his back inner gorge
memories trickling from behind.

Blue sky brilliance fall day
sun crackling the desert
evaporating earth's memory-
pre-dawn deep pocket
storm clouds spilling rain.

We weave our way through
the canyon, teenagers and adults
life jackets, water
pockets full of snacks.

Black Hole a slit in the canyon
ankle deep water knee deep water
steadily rising trumpeting
a wall of water rushing pushing
everything into our path
scrambling up ledges to higher ground.

Last in line I slip fall into a cove
roiling frigid flood waters
swirling around me
six life jackets knotted braided
cast out to me
on the fifth try I latch on
but soon the faces
of my father sister brother
slip away with each tear in the seam
I can feel my sousaphone wrapped
around my body the vibrating horn
the flaring bell still above water
playing my final notes
I am a fish praying for the hook.

www.ingramcontent.com/pod-product-compliance
Lightning Source LLC
Chambersburg PA
CBHW040307170426
43194CB00022B/2933